WHAT YOU NEED TO KNOW ABOUT
ALLERGIES

BY NANCY DICKMANN

raintree
a Capstone company — publishers for children

Raintree is an imprint of Capstone Global Library Limited, a company incorporated in England and Wales having its registered office at 264 Banbury Road, Oxford, OX2 7DY – Registered company number 6695582

www.raintree.co.uk
myorders@raintree.co.uk

Produced by Brown Bear Books Ltd
Design Manager: Keith Davis
Editors: Dawn Titmus, Tracey Kelly
Editorial Director: Lindsey Lowe
Children's Publisher: Anne O'Daly
Picture Manager: Sophie Mortimer
Medical Consultants: Marjorie J. Hogan, MD; Kristina Routh, MB ChB, MP
Printed and bound in China

ISBN: 978-1-4747-1169-2
20 19 18 17 16
10 9 8 7 6 5 4 3 2 1

British Library Cataloguing-in-Publication Data
A full catalogue record for this book is available from the British Library.

Photo Credits
Front Cover: Shutterstock: Brian A. Jackson (top), Evan Lome (bottom).
Inside: 1, © Shutterstock/Jarek Chabraszewski. 3, © Shutterstock/Vit-plus. 5 (top), © Thinkstock/istockphoto. 5 (bottom), © Thinkstock/Monkey Business Images. 6 (top), © Thinkstock/Vladyslav Danilin. 6 (bottom), © Shutterstock/Evgeniya Tiplyashina. 7, © Thinkstock/microphoto. 8, © Shutterstock/K Zenon. 9, © Shutterstock/Panya Kuanun. 10, © Shutterstock/WaveBreakMedia. 11 (top), © Shutterstock/Monkey Business Images. 11 (bottom), © Shutterstock/ProStockStudio. 12, © Shutterstock/Marco Govel. 13, © Shutterstock/Monkey Business Images. 14, © Shutterstock/Volosina. 16, © Shutterstock/Photographee.eu. 17, © Shutterstock/ Daren Baker. 18, © Shutterstock/Arvind Balaraman. 19, © Shutterstock/Adriatic Photo. 20, © Thinkstock/Mike Watson Images. 21, © Shutterstock. 22, © Science Photo Library/Dr Jeremy Burgess. 23, © Science Photo Library/Amelie-Benoist/BSIP. 24, © Science Photo Library/Clouds Hill Imaging Ltd. 25, © Shutterstock/Yarek Gora. 26, © Shutterstock/WaveBreakMedia. 27, © Thinkstock/Elena Thewis. 28, © Shutterstock/Andrey Valerevich. 29, © Thinkstock/istockphoto.

Brown Bear Books has made every attempt to contact the copyright holder.
If anyone has any information please contact licensing@brownbearbooks.co.uk

CONTENTS

Chapter 1
What are allergies? 4

Chapter 2
Testing for allergies 12

Chapter 3
Treating allergies 18

Chapter 4
Living with allergies 24

Glossary 30
Find out more 31
Index 32

Some words are shown in bold, **like this**.
You can find out what they mean by looking in the glossary.

CHAPTER 1
WHAT ARE ALLERGIES?

Do you know someone who starts to sneeze and itch when he or she is outside on a spring day? Or maybe someone whose eyes get watery when he or she is near a cat? You probably have a friend who can't eat certain foods, such as peanuts. All of these reactions are examples of allergies.

▲ In the United Kingdom, hay fever affects up to 30 per cent of adults.

▲ In the United Kingdom, hay fever affects up to 20 per cent of children.

▲ Allergies that cause the skin to react affect about 16 per cent of children in the United Kingdom.

▲ Food allergies affect about 8 per cent of children in the United Kingdom.

◄ The pollen from this beautiful field of flowers can make an allergy sufferer feel completely awful.

Your body has a network called the **immune system**, which helps to keep you healthy. It works by finding and killing germs that might make you ill. However, sometimes the immune system can get things wrong. When you have an allergy, the immune system is **triggered** by harmless substances such as **pollen** or some foods. It reacts as though they were dangerous germs.

► People with food allergies have to be careful about what they eat.

immune system – the system that protects the body by finding and destroying germs

trigger – cause something to begin. Certain substances can trigger allergic reactions.

pollen – the fine powder made by a plant's flowers. Pollen can trigger allergic reactions in some people.

◀ Some people are allergic to shellfish, such as shrimp, lobster and crab.

TYPES OF ALLERGIES

There are many types of allergies. Any substance that causes an allergic reaction is called an **allergen**. Allergens can be breathed in, eaten, injected or touched. Some people may be allergic to only one thing, and others may be allergic to several.

▶ Tiny flakes of dead skin on a cat or dog can cause an allergic reaction in some people.

Grace loved animals, so when she found out that she was allergic to cats and dogs, she was very upset. Since then, she has found that some types of dogs don't trigger her allergies. She now has a poodle as a pet. These dogs are hypoallergenic, meaning they shed less hair and produce less saliva than most other breeds of dog.

Allergies are often grouped into types. The most common allergies are triggered by breathing in substances found in the air, such as mould, dust or pollen. Food allergies are triggered by eating certain foods. Skin allergies involve allergens, such as detergents or perfumes, coming into contact with the skin. Insect allergies cause reactions when you are bitten or stung. Some people are allergic to medicines, such as penicillin.

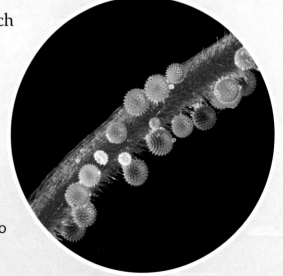

▶ Pollen grains are too tiny to see without a microscope.

allergen – a substance that causes an allergic reaction

ALLERGY SYMPTOMS

Depending on the type of allergy, it can cause very different **symptoms**. Many allergens that are breathed in, such as the pollen that triggers hay fever, can make people sneeze. Allergens can also cause a stuffy or runny nose and runny eyes.

▲ Pollen can cause sneezing. The symptoms of some allergies are similar to those of a cold.

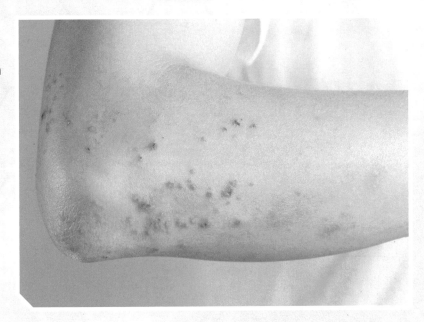

▶ Some allergies can cause a raised, itchy rash called hives.

Other types of allergies, including food allergies, can make the mouth feel tingly and itchy. They can also cause shortness of breath, problems with swallowing, and swelling or itching of the face and other areas. Nausea, vomiting and diarrhoea can also be caused by food allergies. Skin allergies often cause itchy, painful rashes. One of the most serious types of reaction is called **anaphylaxis**. This is a sudden, severe reaction to an allergen and must be treated immediately.

symptom – something different you notice about your body, suggesting that there is an illness or health problem

asthma – disease of the lungs that makes it difficult to breathe

anaphylaxis – an extreme allergic reaction to a substance

WHAT CAUSES ALLERGIES?

You cannot catch allergies from someone else, like you catch a cold. You may be born with allergies, or they may develop later in life. Some people eventually grow out of their allergies, but others will stay allergic for their whole lives.

▼ You don't need to worry about catching allergies from your friends.

▲ Sometimes allergies run in families.

More and more people are being diagnosed with allergies, but scientists still aren't sure why some people have them and others don't. If your parents have allergies, then you are more likely to have them too. But some people with allergic parents have no allergies at all. Many scientists believe that being exposed to certain substances, especially at an early age, can lead to allergies. Others believe it helps to prevent them from developing.

▶ Some scientists think that we have become so good at getting rid of germs that it is causing more allergies.

CHAPTER 2

TESTING FOR ALLERGIES

It is not always easy to tell if you have an allergy. Many of the symptoms of allergies can be caused by other things. For example, a stuffy or runny nose and coughing can be caused by a cold. Rashes can be caused by nettle stings or many other conditions.

▼ If one of your symptoms is a fever, you might have a cold or the flu instead of an allergy.

▲ Keeping a diary of your symptoms will help
your doctor to pinpoint what the problem is.

If you think you have an allergy, you should talk
to your doctor. It might help if you keep a diary of your
symptoms first. Write down what your symptoms are,
when they happen and how severe they are. If you also
keep a record of what you eat and what you come into
contact with, you might start to see a pattern. If you keep
getting a rash, you might discover that it usually happens
after eating a certain food. A rash may also happen after
touching animals or using a certain lotion or shampoo.

TYPES OF TESTS

There are so many allergens that working out which one is causing your symptoms can be a tricky job. A doctor will ask a lot of questions about your medical history. He or she will also ask how and when your symptoms occur.

Often, the next step in diagnosing allergies is performing a skin test. In this kind of testing, the doctor or nurse will use a needle to scratch or inject tiny amounts of an allergen into your skin. Your doctor or nurse can test for dozens of possible allergens at the same time. The amounts used are so small that the testing is very safe. The doctor or nurse will watch for possible signs of a severe reaction. If you are allergic to any of the substances tested, redness or swelling should appear within 15 to 20 minutes.

▲ Peanuts and tree nuts are just one example of the allergens that can be used in a skin test.

Skin Testing

1. The doctor asks questions and checks your general health.

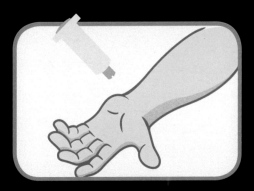

2. The doctor or nurse pricks or scratches a tiny drop of a possible allergen onto the skin.

3. The doctor or nurse pricks other possible allergens onto the skin and keeps track of what went where.

4. You wait for 15 minutes.

5. Any pricks that cause an itchy red bump indicate an allergic reaction.

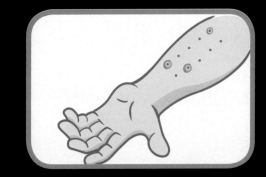

BLOOD TESTS

Skin tests are usually the most effective way to find out what you're allergic to, but sometimes a doctor or nurse will do a blood test instead. Blood tests are useful for patients who are taking medicines that might interfere with a skin test. Other problems, such as a heart condition, might make blood tests safer than skin testing.

HEALTH FACT

Blood tests usually screen for several of the most common allergens, including dust, trees, weeds and moulds. They can also be used for food allergies.

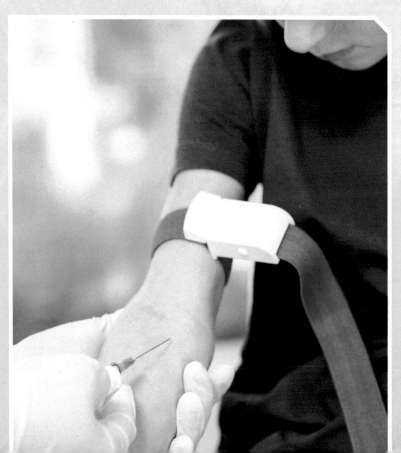

◄ A doctor or nurse will use a needle to take a small amount of blood from your arm.

When you come into contact with an allergen, your body makes substances called **antibodies** to fight it. The antibodies tell your cells to release certain chemicals. An allergy blood test involves using a needle to take some of your blood. The blood is then tested in a lab to see if any antibodies are present.

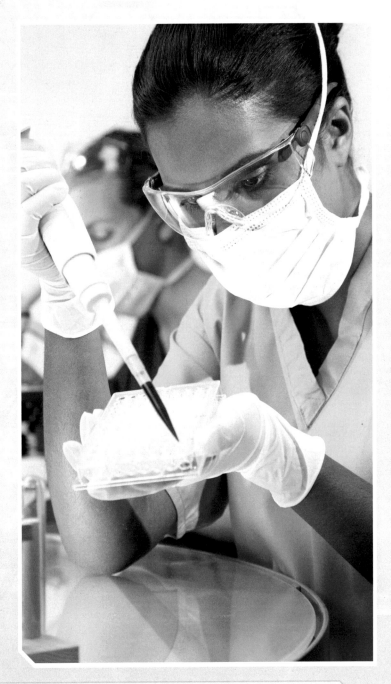

▶ Blood samples have to be analysed in a lab, so it may be up to two weeks before the results are ready.

antibody – substance produced by the body to fight disease

CHAPTER 3

TREATING ALLERGIES

Unfortunately, there is no cure for allergies. Allergies are common in children. Some children eventually grow out of them, but other people have allergies for the rest of their lives. One way to treat allergies is with medicines that make the symptoms less severe. But one of the best ways of dealing with allergies is to avoid exposure to the allergens that trigger them.

◀ Many people who have allergies need medication to control their symptoms.

Say you are allergic to a certain type of food, such as eggs. In this case, you can take steps to avoid eating them or coming into contact with them. But if you are allergic to pollen or mould in the air, it is impossible to avoid them completely. For people who have these types of allergies, treatment focuses on ways to make their symptoms less severe.

◀ Just as there are many different types of allergies, there are also many different treatments too.

eczema – a skin condition that causes redness, itching and scaly or crusty sores

ANTIHISTAMINES AND STEROIDS

Several medications are used to treat allergies, depending on the type of allergy. The most common type is called **antihistamine**. During an allergic reaction, the body releases a chemical called histamine. It can make airways become narrow and blood vessels widen, causing swelling and itching. Antihistamine medications work to block the histamine and reduce the symptoms.

▲ With treatment, most people with allergies can live normal lives.

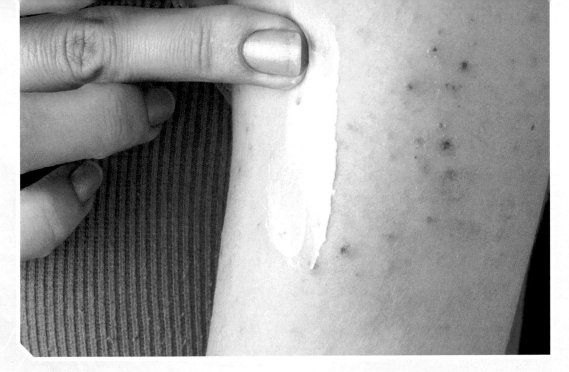

▲ Steroid creams can help treat allergy flare-ups by reducing inflammation.

Antihistamines can be taken before being exposed to an allergen or after a reaction has started. They can be taken in many forms, including tablets, creams, syrups, nasal sprays and eye drops.

Steroids are another common medication used to treat allergies. They can help reduce swelling and inflammation. When steroids are inhaled by someone with allergic asthma, they reduce swelling of the airways. Steroids can also be used as creams to treat skin allergies.

antihistamine – type of drug used to treat allergies by blocking histamine

steroid – substance that reduces inflammation and swelling

IMMUNOTHERAPY

Another treatment for allergies is called **immunotherapy**. Antihistamines help to treat the symptoms of an allergic reaction, but immunotherapy works in a different way. Its goal is to make the body's immune system less sensitive to allergens. This makes allergic reactions less severe.

▲ Bee stings can be deadly for some people, but immunotherapy can help reduce the risk.

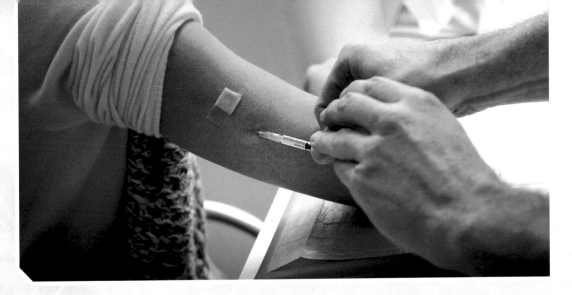

▲ Some people refer to immunotherapy treatment as allergy injections.

In immunotherapy, a tiny amount of an allergen is injected into the patient's arm. Sometimes it is given as a tablet or spray. Over time these doses are repeated, getting slightly larger each time. The patient waits at the clinic for an hour after the injection, in case it causes a reaction. Immunotherapy teaches the immune system to tolerate the allergen rather than fighting it. A course of immunotherapy usually lasts for at least two years.

Immunotherapy cannot be used for all types of allergies. It can help people with severe hay fever or those who are allergic to insect stings, but it cannot yet help with eczema. Scientists are working on ways to use immunotherapy to help people with food allergies.

immunotherapy – a way of treating allergies that involves exposing the patient to tiny doses of the allergen

CHAPTER 4

LIVING WITH ALLERGIES

Learning to live with an allergy can be difficult, but people do it every day. The strongest weapon you have against allergies is knowledge! Knowing what sets off your allergies can help you to work out ways to avoid the trigger or triggers.

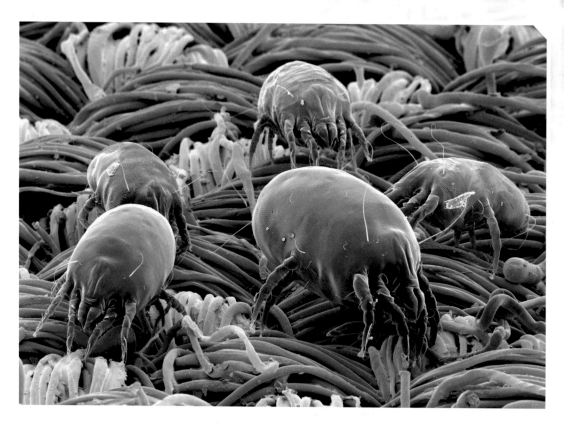

▲ Dust mites are too small to see without a microscope, but their droppings are a common allergen.

Simple actions around the home can help people who are allergic to dust, mould and pets. Regular vacuuming and cleaning can keep dust and pet **dander** under control. Wood floors instead of rugs and carpets, especially in bedrooms, reduce dust too. Using a dehumidifier to dry out the air will help to prevent the growth of mould.

▶ The tiny flakes of dead skin that a dog sheds are called dander. Some dog breeds, such as the wheaten terrier, produce less dander, so they are better for people with allergies.

dander – flaky scales of skin or fur that can cause allergic reactions

MANAGING FOOD ALLERGIES

Living with a food allergy can be a daily battle for some people. Common allergens such as milk and eggs are found in a huge variety of prepared foods. And some foods, such as peanuts, can cause extremely serious reactions, even if the person only comes into contact with a tiny amount of them.

▶ Reading food labels can help you to avoid common food allergens.

Anaphylaxis Warning Signs

- Itchy skin or raised, red rash
- Swelling of the lips, eyes, mouth, tongue, hands or feet
- Feeling light-headed
- Wheezing or breathing difficulties
- Nausea or vomiting
- If you think that someone is experiencing anaphylaxis, call 999 right away.

People with food allergies must read food labels carefully. By law, common allergens in any packaged food must be clearly labelled. Restaurants, cafés and other food outlets have to tell you about allergens if you ask. Sometimes contact with food allergens causes anaphylaxis.

People with severe food allergies should carry a special **auto-injection pen** with an automatic needle, so that they can inject themselves with emergency medicine. They should keep a pen at every place they regularly visit.

▲ A special pen-like device injects medicine into a person's thigh to stop anaphylaxis.

▶ If you visit a friend, make sure their parents know about any food allergies you have.

auto-injection pen – a device that can inject emergency allergy medication into a patient

MANAGING SKIN ALLERGIES

Red, itchy rashes are a common symptom of allergies. They can be triggered when your skin comes into contact with an allergen. But rashes can also be a reaction to other triggers, such as something that you ate. The rashes can blister and bleed, causing pain and discomfort.

▲ Knowing what triggers your allergies can help you to plan activities that won't cause a reaction.

Ali was experiencing sneezing and itching, even when it wasn't hay fever season. He kept a record of his allergy symptoms for two weeks to show his doctor. A skin test showed that he was allergic to mould. He and his family worked hard to reduce the mould in their home, and his symptoms improved.

Lotions and medicated creams can help to make rashes less painful. Warm baths to keep the skin full of moisture can also help. Using natural or hypoallergenic beauty products, which have no dyes or perfumes, is one way to avoid allergens.

For most people, allergies can be managed by using medication prescribed by a doctor and limiting their exposure to allergens.

▶ If you have skin allergies, look for sunscreens that are hypoallergenic.

GLOSSARY

allergen substance that causes an allergic reaction

anaphylaxis extreme allergic reaction to a substance

antibody substance produced by the body to fight disease

antihistamine type of drug used to treat allergies by blocking histamine

asthma disease of the lungs that makes it difficult to breathe

auto-injection pen device that can inject emergency allergy medication into a patient

dander flaky scales of skin or fur that can cause allergic reactions

eczema skin condition that causes redness, itching and scaly or crusty sores

immune system system that protects the body by finding and destroying germs

immunotherapy way of treating allergies that involves exposing the patient to tiny doses of the allergen

pollen fine powder made by a plant's flowers. Pollen can trigger allergic reactions in some people.

steroid substance that reduces inflammation and swelling

symptom something different you notice about your body, suggesting there is a health problem

trigger cause something to begin. Certain substances can trigger allergic reactions.

BOOKS

Food Allergies and Me: A Children's Book, Juniper Skinner (CreateSpace, 2010).

James and the Big Battle: A Children's Book About Allergies, Jen Burns (CreateSpace, 2014).

The Allergy-free Family Cookbook: 100 Delicious Recipes Free from Dairy, Eggs, Peanuts, Tree Nuts, Soya, Gluten, Sesame and Shellfish, Fiona Heggie and Ellie Lux (Orion, 2015).

Tom, Rosie and the Battle of the Allergy, Anet Shabi (CreateSpace, 2016).

WEBSITES

Allergy UK
Advice and information about the different types of allergies and how to manage them.
www.allergyuk.org/allergy-in-children

NHS Choices
Information about the types of allergies, how to treat them and how to prevent them.
www.nhs.uk/conditions/allergies/pages/introduction.aspx

INDEX

allergy types
   food 4, 5, 7, 9, 16, 23, 26, 27
   insect 7, 22
   medicine 7
   skin 4, 7, 9, 21, 28, 29
allergens
   bee stings 22
   dust mites 7, 16, 25
   eggs 19, 26
   milk 26
   mould 7, 16, 19, 25, 29
   peanuts 4, 14, 26
   pet dander 24, 25
   pollen 5, 7, 8, 19
   shellfish 6
   tree nuts 14
   trees 16
   weeds 16
allergy testing
   blood testing 16, 17
   skin testing 14, 15, 16, 29
anaphylaxis 26, 27
antibodies 17
asthma 8, 9, 19, 21

eczema 19, 23

germs 5, 10, 11

hay fever 4, 8, 23, 29

immune system 5, 10, 22, 23

symptoms
   hives 9
   itching 4, 9, 15, 19, 20, 26, 28
   rashes 4, 9, 12, 13, 26, 28, 29
   redness 14, 19, 28
   runny eyes 4, 8
   sneezing 4, 8, 29
   stuffy and runny nose
      8, 12
   swelling 9, 14, 20, 21, 26
symptoms diary 13

treatments
   antihistamines 20, 21, 22
   auto-injection pens 27
   avoidance 18, 19, 24, 26, 29
   exposure 18, 29
   immunotherapy 22, 23
   steroids 20, 21

WH	8/16